1

HEALING THE SICK IN 5 MINUTES

HOW ANYONE CAN HEAL ANY SICKNESS

FRANCIS K.D. JONAH

TABLE OF CONTENTS

3

INTRODUCTION

Most healings I have performed took less than 5 minutes, a few took longer(less than 10) but the essential thing you need to know is that healing is already provided and we just need to receive. My greatest healing breakthrough was when I received healing from a 10 year ulcer with the 4 simple changes in thought I will outline in this short read of less than 20 pages as it is essential you heal or receive healing quickly. I have taught these thoughts to several people who are having numerous testimonies of instant healings. You will undoubtedly produce such testimonies.

CHAPTER ONE:

THE FOUNDATION

Christian healing is difficult for many. It is not supposed to be so. To heal someone in less than 5 minutes you first need to be born again. That is what gives you healing power freely. This you can do by believing in your heart that Jesus is the Son of God and that he died and rose again for you. Rom 10:9 that if thou shalt confess with thy mouth the Lord Jesus, and shalt believe in thine heart that God hath raised him from the dead, thou shalt be saved.

Rom 10:10 for with the heart man believeth unto righteousness; and with the mouth confession is made unto salvation.

Now that you are born again, God doesn't count your sins against you anymore. 2Co 5:19 To wit, that God was in Christ, reconciling the world unto himself, not imputing their trespasses unto them; and hath committed unto us the word of reconciliation.

The above scripture shows that God doesn't impute our sins against us anymore Rom 5:13 (For until the law sin was in the world: but sin is not imputed when there is no law.

Rom 5:14: Nevertheless death reigned from Adam to Moses, even over them that had not sinned after the similitude of Adam's transgression, who is the figure of him that was to come.

Rom 5:15: But not as the offence, so also is the free gift. For if through the offence of one many be dead, much more the grace of God, and the gift by grace, which is by one man, Jesus Christ, hath abounded unto many.

Rom 5:16: And not as it was by one that sinned, so is the gift: for the judgment was by one to condemnation, but the free gift is of many offences unto justification.

Rom 5:17: For if by one man's offence death reigned by one; much more they which receive abundance of grace and of the gift of righteousness shall reign in life by one, Jesus Christ.)

Since we are under Grace and not under law according to Romans 6: 14, our sins are not imputed or counted against us. We also have the gift of righteousness by faith and not law. (Romans 5:17) Past, present and future sins Jesus has paid the price once and for all. Hebrews 10:12: But this man, after he had offered one sacrifice for sins for ever, sat down on the right hand of God;

Hebrews 10:13: From henceforth expecting till his enemies be made his footstool.

Hebrews 10:14: For by one offering he hath perfected for ever them that are sanctified.

He offered one sacrifice for sin FOREVER. We are thus perfect forever according to the above scriptures. It means we do not sin because the law or God will punish us as some still think but then we do not sin because we love God and appreciate what he has done for us. He made us perfect. (Our spirits) With this foundation of your righteousness, let us make the four thought changes that cause healing in less than 5 minutes. NB: Please read all the above scriptures and the ones to come to ensure you can walk in the revelation to heal.

CHAPTER TWO:

THOUGHT NUMBER ONE

God is not about to heal, he has already provided healing. A lot of Christians think that God can do all things but many do not believe he has done anything. When Jesus died he paid the punishment for our sin and by his stripes we were healed. It means healing was provided when he died for us. Right now healing is available, if you are not healed, it is not because God has not provided it, and it is because you have not received. Do not let the Devil keep you in bondage by sickness. Now that you know healing is already provided, you must understand that you are the one tolerating sickness in your body. 1Pe 2:24: Who his own self bare our sins in his own body on the tree that we, being dead to sins, should live unto righteousness: by whose stripes ye were healed.

Isa_53:5: But he was wounded for our transgressions, he was bruised for our iniquities: the chastisement of our peace was upon him; and with his stripes we are healed. Notice the scripture in 1st Peter says you were healed. Healing is already provided. Stop begging God to heal you, he has already provided healing. He is not the factor preventing your healing. It is between you and the devil now. You did not do anything before Jesus died and provided healing. It is free. Receive it and stop thinking it is about your works.

CHAPTER THREE:

THOUGHT NUMBER TWO

You have authority over sickness given to you freely: fasting and prayer doesn't bring authority, it is a free gift.

The day I taught a group of people this truth, they began healing others effortlessly. All along they thought they had to do something to have the authority to heal. Yet they had that authority all along after being born again. Mat 10:1: And when he had called unto him his twelve disciples, he gave them power against unclean spirits, to cast them out, and to heal all manner of sickness and all manner of disease.

Jesus just gave them the authority; they didn't pray or ask for it. He gave it freely to them. They went out with it and came with several testimonies. Every born again person has the same authority over sickness as we speak. Power to heal has been given, if you are not using it, it is because you do not know you have it. Luke 10:19: Behold, I give unto you power to tread on serpents and scorpions, and over all the power of the enemy: and nothing shall by any means hurt you.

Jesus gave power unto us freely. No work done. Power over all the works of the enemy. The disciples of John asked Jesus why his disciples do not fast or pray but the disciples of John and the Pharisees fasted and prayed always. Luke 5:33 And they said unto him, Why do the

disciples of John fast often, and make prayers, and
likewise the disciples of the Pharisees; but thine eat and
drink?

This shows that at the time the disciples were healing all
diseases, they never prayed or fasted. They just used the
authority given to them freely by Jesus. Contrast that to
the disciples of John and the disciples of the Pharisees;
even though they fasted and prayed there were no
healings in their life. It was about the authority given
freely, not the fasting and prayer. The authority is given
to you freely, receive it by faith. How? Thank God you
have it and use it. Simple as that.

CHAPTER FOUR:

THOUGHT NUMBER THREE

Do not ask God to heal you, he already has, command the sickness to go.

A lot of people cry and weep, "God heal me". You won't receive healing that way. And if you pray for someone and say God heal him or her it is the same thing. What you need to do is to let the sickness or disease, be it cancer or arthritis or pains in the stomach or the leg know that your healing is already provided. You thus command it to go and loose its hold of your body. It has no other option than to go because it recognises spiritual authority. Sickness recognises spiritual authority and you have that authority. Mark 11:23: For verily I say unto you, That whosoever shall say unto this mountain, Be thou removed, and be thou cast into the sea; and shall not doubt in his heart, but shall believe that those things which he saith shall come to pass; he shall have whatsoever he saith.

Mark 11:24: **Therefore I say unto you, what things soever ye desire, when ye pray, believe that ye receive them, and ye shall have them.**

The Bible says in the scripture above that you must speak to the mountain. Command it and it will obey you and know you have already received and that is when you will receive. Not receive physically before you

17

know you have received but receive before it manifests

physically.

CHAPTER FIVE:

THOUGHT NUMBER FOUR

Thank God for healing and other things because they are already yours in the Spirit. That is how you acknowledge receipt.

When you acknowledge you have it in the spirit, it manifests physically. Do not wait for physical manifestation before you acknowledge you have received healing. That is not what the word says. Philippians 1:3: Blessed be the God and Father of our Lord Jesus Christ, who hath blessed us with all spiritual blessings in heavenly places in Christ:

Notice that you are already blessed with all spiritual blessings in heaven. That is why we do not pray for blessing but we thank God for already blessing us. That is the way we give place for physical manifestation. You are already blessed. Glory to God now it is time to apply the thought changes for healing.

CHAPTER SIX:

YOU ARE READY TO HEAL OTHERS OR RECEIVE HEALING

Healing others

What I do;

I teach the people that they are already healed if I have time. If I do not have time I go to step two especially those who come to me for prayer.

I pray for them by commanding the sickness or pain by name to go in the name of Jesus. (E.g. I command stomach pain to go right now in Jesus name)

I loose the person from the sickness or pain. (E.g. I loose you from that pain right now in Jesus name).

I thank God for the physical manifestation

Almost immediately, most testify of instant healing.

You can also do same

Receiving healing (or praying for yourself)

Understand healing is already given.

Command the pain or sickness to leave you. (E.g. I command stomach pain to go right now in Jesus name)

Loose yourself from the sickness or pain. (E.g. I loose myself from that pain right now in Jesus name).

Thank God for the physical manifestation

22

Almost immediately, you will testify of instant

healing.

Study the scriptures over again and you will find

yourself looking for people to heal.

CHAPTER SEVEN

TESTIMONIES

Revelation 12:11: *And they overcame him by the blood of the Lamb, and by the word of their testimony; and they loved not their lives unto the death.*

It's important for us to know that the devil don't like it when we get healed and free from his devices. And guess what, he also feels like his still in charge when believers are not bold enough to share the good ness of God in their lives.

Testimonies changes lives. It changes how we think and what we do and what we say. When one receives a testimony of truth, it immediately begins to have impact on that person's life.

Testimonies can serve as the foundation of faith for most people. The reason why the devil feel comfortable when you don't share your testimonies is because he knows he can attack others who don't know what you know. But he gets uncomfortable and defeated when you share your testimonies with other.

WHAT TESTIMONIES DOES!

Testimonies helps to build up the faith of others who are suffering from different forms of illness, sickness and diseases. For instance, if you share someone tells you that he or she was having HIV?AIDS let's say two months ago but he is now healed and free due to his encounter with Jesus Christ. Let's assume you are having headache, stomach pain, malaria, cancer, etc. and you hear such testimonies, automatically, your faith will be lifted. You will be saying or thinking stuffs like, if God can heal him or her, then He can heal me too.

TESTIMONY!

A daughter of mine in my ministry was having a heart problem that troubled her for years. One day I received a call that she was seriously down. When I enquired about what was happening I was told she was having a serious pain in her heart and that her drug has finished.

I could not drive down to her place as of the time I was called because I was very far off. But I asked the person that called me to lay hands on her and I asked him to command the pain to go and never return. To the glory of God, she received her healing.

Take note: she has being living with that pain and on drugs for years before she joined my ministry. When she shared her testimony to the rest of the congregation, she said her father sends her drugs in monthly bases. But that day there was no drug. She also said her father wanted her to pick the next bus and return home for proper medical care. But she decided to wait and call me. Just as you will expect, she is no longer having that pain and she is no longer living on drugs.

I decree that every sick in your life disappears now in the name of Jesus. Receive it now.

NOW IT'S YOUR TURN!

Your testimony can save a life.

You can send us a mail with your testimonies on how this book have either helped you receive healing or heal someone. You are blessed.

My email is

drfrancisjonah@gmail.com

PRAYER OF SALVATION:

The greatest miracle is not that eyes was opened, the deaf heard, Heart pain disappeared, the dead was raised, debt was cleared or you bought a house or car etc.

*The greatest miracle is **SALVATION.***

*The greatest miracle happens when you give your life to Jesus. The bible said in **2corinthians 5:17;** **"Therefore if any man be in Christ, he is a new creature: old things are passed away; behold, all things are become new"***

The moment you give your life to Jesus Christ, every negative thin in your life comes to an end. If you have not met Jesus, I want to pray specially for you.

Just pray this prayer after me;

"Lord Jesus Christ, I come to you today as a sinner, I cannot help myself. Please forgive me of all my sins, I believe in my heart that you died for me and you were raised up by God.

Today, I accept you Lord Jesus Christ as my lord and saviour.

Cleanse me with your precious blood; deliver me from sin to serve the living God. Thank you Jesus for saving me. Now I know that I am born again in Jesus name... Amen"

If you have said the above prayer,

congratulations; you are born again and your life will not remain the same anymore.

You can write to me at;

drfrancisjonah@gmail.com for prayers and counselling, you are blessed.

30

Other books by FRANCIS JONAH you must read:

- ➢ Be happy now: no more depression

- ➢ Achieve something now

- ➢ Healing the sick in 5 minutes

- ➢ The healing miracle prayer

- ➢ The financial miracle prayer

- ➢ Powerful prayer method for all prayers

- ➢ Multiply your personal income in less than 30 days

- ➢ Finding happiness: the john miller story

- ➢ The power of faith-filled words

- ➢ How to overcome sin effortlessly

32

Printed in Great Britain
by Amazon

47400355R00020